Conversations for Work

Ellen Vacco
Paula Jablon

New Readers Press

Conversations for Work
ISBN 978-1-56420-587-2

Copyright © 2007 New Readers Press
New Readers Press
A Publishing Division of ProLiteracy
1320 Jamesville Avenue, Syracuse, New York 13210
www.newreaderspress.com

Printed in the United States of America
9 8 7 6 5 4 3

All proceeds from the sale of New Readers Press materials
support literacy programs in the United States and worldwide.

Developmental Editor: Paula L. Schlusberg
Creative Director: Andrea Woodbury
Illustrations: Roger Audette represented by Wilkinson Studios Inc. and Brian Wallace, Wilkinson Studios
Production Specialist: Jeffrey R. Smith
Cover Design: James Wallace

Contents

To the Student

Conversations for Work will help you
- understand your boss
- understand other people at work
- speak to your boss
- speak to other people at work
- learn about working in the U.S.

At the end of this book, there are useful words and expressions for work. There is also a place for you to write your own words.

To the Teacher

The Teacher's Guide that accompanies *Conversations For Work* contains suggestions for use of lesson materials, including numerous expansion activities. The photocopy masters in the Teacher's Guide provide additional oral and written exercises designed to reinforce and enhance the material in the student book.

Unit One   People and Places at Work

Lesson 1 Starting a New Job

Rosa has a new job. She is a housekeeper.
Rosa talks to her boss. Listen to the conversation.

Boss: Hi, Rosa. I'm Ms. Robbins. It's nice to meet you.
Rosa: It's nice to meet you, too.
Boss: Rosa, I need some information.
Rosa: OK.
Boss: Can you please spell your last name?
Rosa: G-O-M-E-Z
Boss: Where do you live?
Rosa: 36 Main Street, Los Angeles
Boss: What is your phone number?
Rosa: 818-555-6339
Boss: Thanks, Rosa.

Do you give information at work?

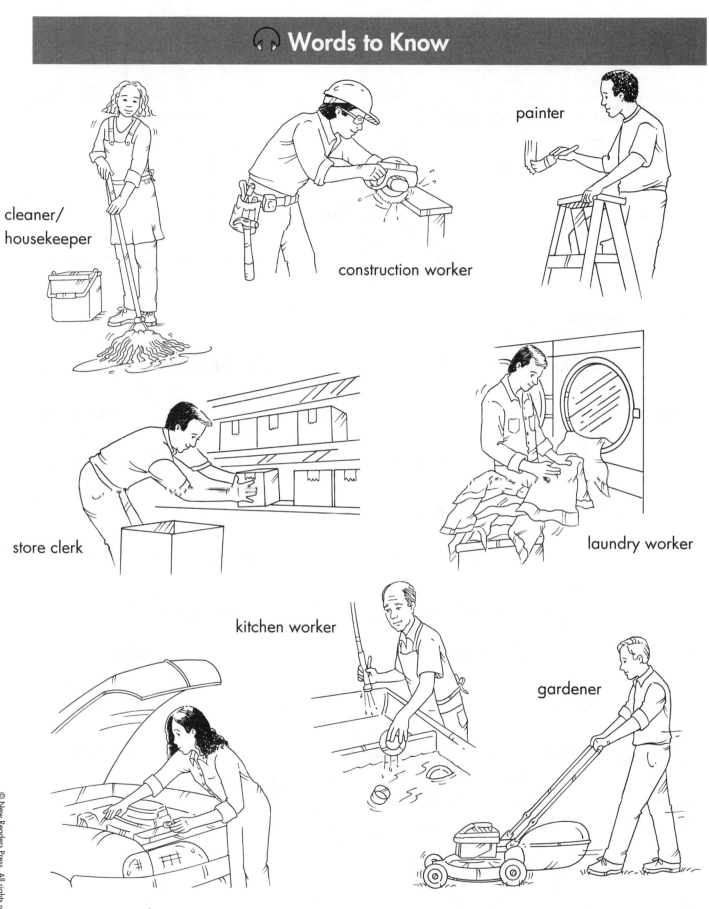

cleaner/
housekeeper

construction worker

painter

store clerk

laundry worker

kitchen worker

gardener

mechanic

Unit 1 People and Places at Work **7**

Full Form		Contraction	Full Form		Contraction
I	am	(I'm)	we	are	(we're)
you	are	(you're)	you	are	(you're)
he		(he's)			
she	} is	(she's)	they	are	(they're)
it		(it's)			

Complete the sentences.

Use the full form.   **Use the contraction.**

Example: I _____*am*_____ a gardener.   Example: _____*I'm*_____ a gardener.

1. He _____ a laundry worker.   _____ a laundry worker.

2. They _____ dishwashers.   _____ dishwashers.

3. We _____ meat packers.   _____ meat packers.

4. She _____ 32 years old.   _____ 32 years old.

5. It _____ Tuesday.   _____ Tuesday.

6. I _____ a taxi driver.   _____ a taxi driver.

7. You _____ a good friend.   _____ a good friend.

8. He _____ a mechanic.   _____ a mechanic.

Oral Practice

I. **What is your job?** _____
   What are other jobs? Make a list with your class.

   daycare worker   _____   _____

II. **Answer the questions. Practice the conversation.**

   A. What is your name?

   B. _____

   A. Please spell your last name.

   B. ____ ____ ____ ____ ____ ____ ____ ____ ____

   A. What is your address?

   B. _____

   A. Please spell the name of your street.

   B. ____ ____ ____ ____ ____ ____ ____ ____ ____

   A. What is your phone number?

   B. (____) ____ - _____

   A. Where do you work?

   B. _____

   A. What is your job?

   B. _____

Listening Practice

🎧 **Listen to the questions. Write your answers.**

1. What is your zip code? _____

2. What is your area code? _____

3. What is your date of birth? _____

4. What is your phone number at work? _____

Let's think about it.

🎧 **Listen to the story. Answer the questions with your class.**

My name is Yuri. I'm from Russia. In my native country I was a teacher. In the U.S. I work in a supermarket. I'm happy to have a job. But I want to be a teacher again.

- What is your job in the U.S.?
  Do you like it?
  Explain.

- What was your job in your native country?
  Did you like it?
  Explain.

Application

1. **What is the name of your department?** _____
   Name other departments at work. Make a list with your class.

   _____maintenance_____   _____   _____

   _____   _____   _____

2. **Ask a partner these questions. Write your partner's information.**

   • What is your name? _____

   • Where do you live? _____

   • Where do you work? _____

   • What is your department? _____

Now tell the class about your partner.

   • His/Her name is _____

   • He/She lives in _____

   • He/She works at _____

   • He/She works in the _____ department.

Lesson 2   Finding Places at Work

 Sam works in a hospital. His boss gives him directions to the coffee shop. Listen to the conversation.

Boss: Please take these supplies to the coffee shop.

Sam: Where's the coffee shop?

Boss: On the first floor.

Sam: Is it near the lobby?

Boss: No, it's near the kitchen, across from the restrooms.

Sam: The coffee shop is on the first floor, near the kitchen, across from the restrooms. Is that right?

Boss: That's right.

Can you find places at work?

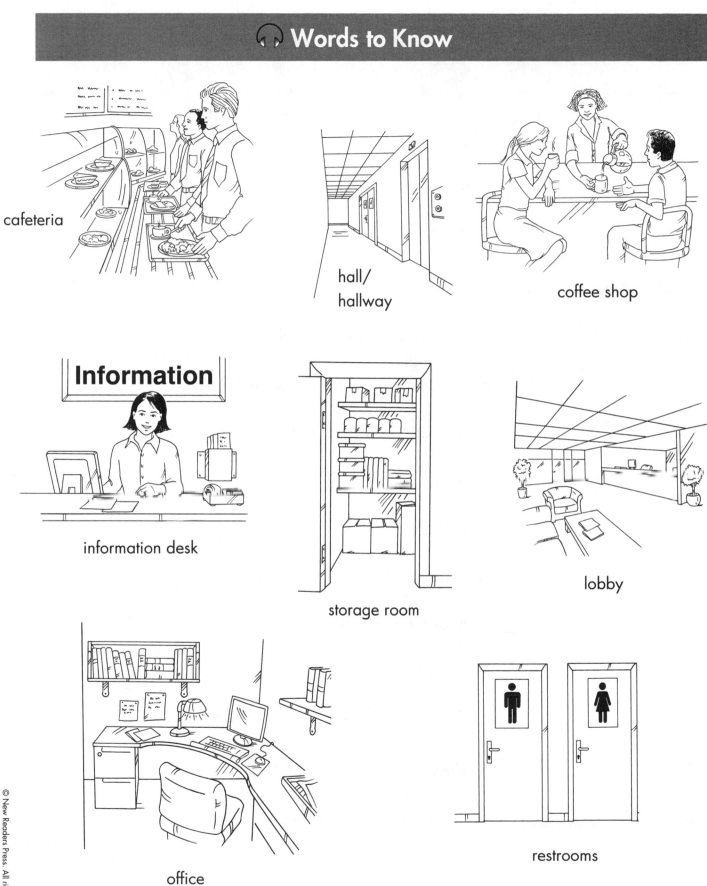

cafeteria

hall/
hallway

coffee shop

information desk

storage room

lobby

office

restrooms

Am	I		Are	we
Are	you		Are	you
Is	{ he		Are	they
	she			
	it			

Complete the questions.

Example: _____ Is _____ the telephone in the lobby?

1. _____ the restrooms near the coffee shop?

2. _____ the cafeteria across from the office?

3. _____ you in the basement?

4. _____ Max and Luis in the break room?

5. _____ the soda machine on the first floor?

6. _____ we near the cafeteria?

7. _____ Sonya in the office?

8. _____ the storage room next to the kitchen?

9. _____ the elevator down the hall?

10. _____ the stairs near the elevator?

I. Look at the map. What do you see?

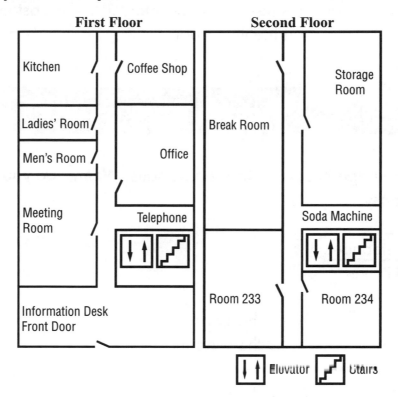

II. Practice the conversation.

A. Where's the _____(a)_____?

B. It's on the first/second floor, _____(b)_____.

(a) break room
telephone
information desk
soda machine
kitchen
elevator

_____

_____

(b) near the storage room
across from the meeting room
near the front door
next to the storage room
across from the coffee shop
next to the stairs

_____

_____

🎧 **III. Say it at work.**

a. It's down the hall, on the right.
Open the door.
Turn on the light.

b. Where's the office?
Near room number 4.
It's next to the elevator, on the third floor.

c. Is the lab in the basement?
No, it's on the first floor.
Go upstairs and turn left.
There's a sign on the door.

Listening Practice

🎧 **Look at the map on page 15. Listen to the directions. Where are you? Circle the correct answer.**

Example: **a.** the telephone
        b. the kitchen

1. **a.** the ladies' room
   b. the telephone

2. **a.** soda machine
   b. Room 233

3. **a.** the kitchen
   b. the meeting room

4. **a.** the stairs
   b. the soda machine

5. **a.** Room 234
   b. the storage room

6. **a.** the front door
   b. the office

Let's think about it.

🎧 **Listen to the story. Answer the questions with your class.**

Stella works in a hospital. Visitors ask her questions. They say, "Where are the restrooms?" and "How do I get to the coffee shop?" Stella only speaks a little English. She smiles and says, "I'm sorry. I don't understand. They can help you at the Information Desk. It's on the first floor."

- Visitors ask Stella questions. What does she say?

- Do people ask you questions at work? What do you say?

Application

1. **Make a list of the places you go at work.**

   <u> break room </u>   _____   _____

   _____   _____   _____

2. **Make questions about places at work. Answer the questions with your class.**

   Where is the _____ at work?

break room	HR office	restroom
cafeteria/lunchroom	supply room	telephone

Lesson 3   Understanding the Job

Angela works in a hospital kitchen. Her boss, Mr. Paige, tells her what to do. Listen to the conversation.

Mr. Paige: Sometimes you deliver the meals.

Angela: OK.

Mr. Paige: First, put the meals on the trays. Next, load the trays on the cart. Then, deliver the meals to the rooms. Do you understand?

Angela: Yes, I think so.

Mr. Paige: Good. Please tell me if you don't understand. It's important to do the job right.

Angela: OK, Mr. Paige. Thank you.

Does your boss tell you what to do? Do you always understand?

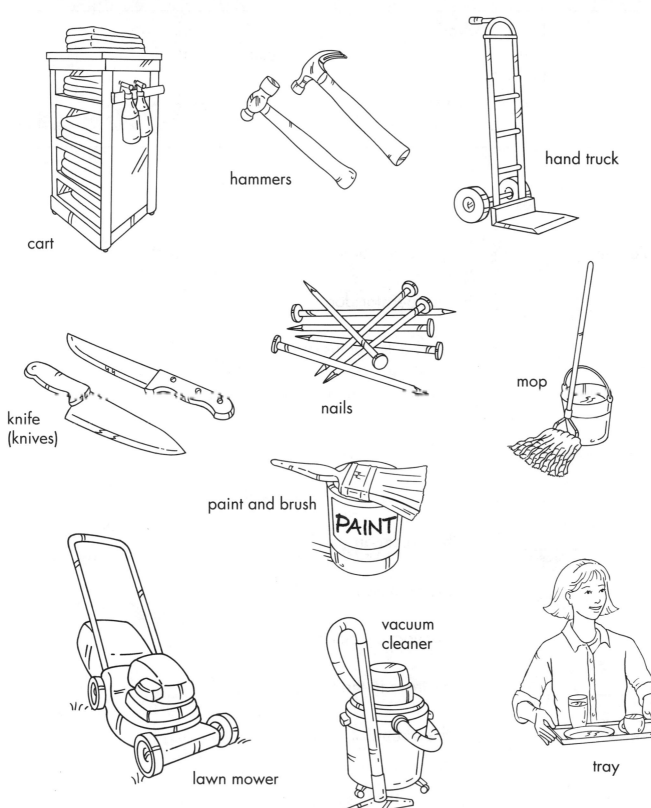

cart

hammers

hand truck

knife (knives)

nails

mop

paint and brush

PAINT

lawn mower

vacuum cleaner

tray

I	work	we	work
you	work	you	work
he			
she }	works	they	work
it			

Complete the sentences.

Example: He _____works_____ every Saturday.
                    (work)

1. I _____ the refrigerator door.
        (open)

2. They _____ knives to cut the meat.
          (use)

3. Pedro _____ boxes on the hand truck.
           (load)

4. I _____ the cart.
       (push)

5. My sister _____ soup at the restaurant.
              (make)

6. Raj _____ the paint can.
        (close)

7. We _____ the hammer.
       (put away)

8. You _____ the vacuum cleaner.
        (turn off)

9. Jim _____ the trays in the kitchen.
        (pick up)

10. We _____ the old nails.
        (throw away)

I. **What tools, equipment, and supplies do you use at work?**
Make a list with your class.

_____   _____   _____

_____   _____   _____

II. **Write sentences. Use the words from your list and the following**
verbs: *get, use, put away, throw away*. (See page 115 for
more verbs.)
Work with your class. Make as many sentences as you can.
Then say the sentences.

Example: I put away the nails.   He gets the lettuce.

_____   _____

_____   _____

_____   _____

_____   _____

_____   _____

III. Say it at work.

a. I don't understand.
I don't understand.
Please say it again.
I don't understand.

b. First I get the mop
and I wash the floor.
Next I put supplies away.
Then I close the door.

c. Please repeat that.
Please say it again.
I want to understand.
Is it two knives or ten?

Let's think about it.

Listen to the story. Answer the questions with your class.

My name is Sergio. I deliver pizzas. My manager talks very fast. Sometimes I don't understand her. I'm afraid to tell my manager that I don't understand. But I don't want to make mistakes. I don't want to lose my job.

- What should Sergio do?

- What do you do when you don't understand?
What do you say?
Explain.

Listening Practice

Listen to the directions. Repeat them in the same order.

Talk about your job.

I am a/an _____. I do many things at work.

(your job)

First I _____.

Next I _____.

Then I _____.

I also _____.

I use _____, _____, _____, and

_____ to do my job.

Sometimes I also use _____ and _____.

Lesson 4 Finding Supplies

Cho and Kim work in the laundry. They get supplies from a supply closet. Listen to the conversation.

Cho: Kim, I need to wash the clothes. But we're out of detergent. Where is a new box of detergent?

Kim: It's in the supply closet.

Cho: I looked in the supply closet. I don't see it.

Kim: It's on the first shelf.

Cho: Is it behind the bleach?

Kim: Yes.

Cho: OK. I'll look again.

Where do you keep supplies at work?

bleach

brushes

cups

sponges

light bulbs

soap

trash bags

paper towels

detergent

toilet paper

| above | below | in | next to |
| behind | between | in front of | on |

Complete the sentences.

1. The hammer is _____ the toolbox.

2. The nails are _____ the toolbox.

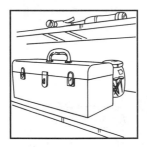

3. The hammer is _____ the toolbox.

4. The nails are _____ the toolboxes.

5. The hammer is _____ the toolbox.

6. The nails are _____ the toolbox.

7. The hammer is _____ the toolbox.

8. The nails are _____ the toolbox.

I. **Look at the supply closet. What do you see?**

II. **Practice the conversation.**

A. Where is/are the _____ (a) _____?

B. On the shelf, _____ (b) _____.

a)	(b)
sponges	above the trash bags
window cleaner	below the trash bags
toilet paper	below the soap
paper towels	between the bleach and the window cleaner
detergent	behind the bleach
brushes	in front of the trash bags
glasses	next to the light bulbs

II. Say it at work.

a. Where's the broom?
Where's the broom?
It's on the floor
in the storage room.

b. Is the meat in the freezer?
Do you see it in there?
It's not on the first shelf.
I looked everywhere.

c. Where is the mop?
I need to wash the floor.
It's in the storage room,
next to the door.

Let's think about it.

Listen to the story. Talk with your class.

My name is Janet. I have a new job in a restaurant. Today I used the dishwasher for the first time. I got detergent from the supply closet. There was a picture of dishes on the bottle. I put this detergent in the dishwasher. But it was the wrong detergent. Soon there were soap bubbles and water all over the floor. What a mess!

- Janet used the wrong detergent because she didn't understand.
  Do you know a story like this?
  Tell the class.

Listening Practice

Look at the supply closet on page 27. Listen to the descriptions. Circle the correct answer.

Example: a. the bleach
(b. the mop)

1. **a.** the sponges
   b. the toilet paper

2. **a.** the bleach
   b. the toilet paper

3. **a.** the soap
   b. the bleach

4. **a.** the light bulbs
   b. the trash bags

Application

1. **What supplies do you use at work? Make a list with your class.**

   _____   _____   _____

   _____   _____   _____

2. **Where do you keep supplies at work?**

cabinet	warehouse	toolbox
shelf	basement	refrigerator/freezer
drawer	storage shed	_____
locker	supply closet	_____

	Yes	No	Sometimes
• I can talk about myself.	____	____	____
• I can talk about my job.	____	____	____
• I tell my boss when I don't understand.	____	____	____
• I can find places at work.	____	____	____
• I can find things at work.	____	____	____

Unit Two   Time and Work

Lesson 5 Understanding a Schedule

Chong talks to the manager about her work schedule. Listen to the conversation.

Chong: Ms. Smith, can you tell me about my work schedule?

Ms. Smith: Yes. You work first shift. Your hours are from 8:00 to 4:30. Lunch is from 12:00 to 12:30. You have two 15-minute breaks.

Chong: What are my days off?

Ms. Smith: Monday and Tuesday. Tell me if you need to change your schedule. I have to find someone to work for you. Do you understand?

Chong: OK, Ms. Smith.

What is your work schedule?

break

SHIFT 1
7:00

SHIFT 1
7:00

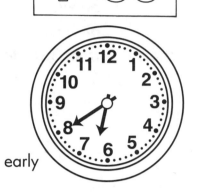
early

late

shift

SHIFT I
7:00 – 3:00

SHIFT II
3:00 – 11:00

SHIFT III
11:00 – 7:00

WORK SCHEDULE

	MON.	TUES.	WED.	THURS.	FRI.	SAT.	SUN.
Alex	9-5	8-4	9-5	8-4	7-3	DAY OFF	1-5 OT
Jose	DAY OFF	10-6	7-3	7-3	9-5	7-3	9-5 OT
Kim	7-3	7-3	7-3	DAY OFF	7-3	DAY OFF	7-3
Peter	9-5	9-5	DAY OFF	7-3	7-3	7-3	DAY OFF
Tamara	8-4	7-3	8-4	7-3	9-5	9-5 OT	DAY OFF

schedule

Sunday	
Monday	
Tuesday	
Wednesday	
Thursday	X
Friday	
Saturday	

time off/day off

today

tonight

vacation

lunch

at with time	*at* 1:00, 4:15, 3:30, etc.
in with months	*in* July, February, etc.
in with years	*in* 1984, 2007, etc.
on with days of the week	*on* Wednesday, Friday, etc
on with dates	*on* June 23, 2008, etc.
from ... to with one time to another	*from* 3:00 *to* 11:00
	from April 6 *to* April 13

Complete the sentences.

Example: I start work _____*at*_____ 7:00.

1. Lunch is _____ 12:00.

2. My hours are _____ 7:00 _____ 3:00.

3. I come in early _____ Saturday.

4. We have a party _____ December.

5. The party is _____ December 23.

6. I work late _____ Friday.

7. My vacation is _____ July 13 _____ July 20.

8. I have a break _____ 10:30 _____ the morning.

9. Miguel was born _____ July 23, 1985.

10. Lin has a day off _____ Tuesday.

Oral Practice

I. Practice the conversation.

A: _____, can I talk to you?

(Your supervisor's name)

B: Sure. What's up?

A: _____(a)_____.

B: _____(b)_____.

A: Thanks a lot.

(a) 1. I'm sick. Can I go home at 3 today?
   2. Can I take vacation from July 6 to July 13?
   3. Can I take Friday off? I have to go to the doctor.
   4. Can I come in at 11 tomorrow?

(b) 1. No problem
   2. I'll get back to you.
   3. I think so. I'll check the schedule.
   4. I'll tell you after lunch.

II. Say it at work.

a. I need time off.
Is it OK?
I'm going to the doctor.
I have an appointment today.

b. Can I talk to you a minute?
My schedule isn't right.
It says I start at 5 o'clock,
but I don't work at night.

c. Can I take my break now?
Can I take my break now?
It's not very busy.
Can I take my break now?

🎧 **I. Listen. Write what you hear.**

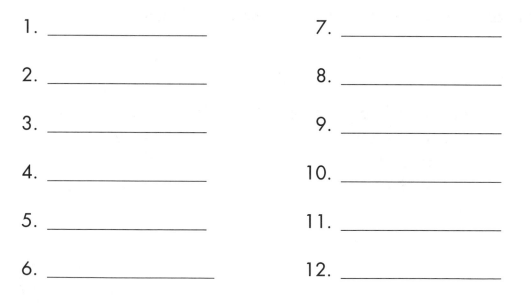

Friday, September 10	
7⁰⁰	
8⁰⁰	
9⁰⁰	
10⁰⁰	
11⁰⁰	
12⁰⁰	
1⁰⁰	
2⁰⁰	
3⁰⁰	
4⁰⁰	
5⁰⁰	
6⁰⁰	
7⁰⁰	

September

Sunday	Monday	Tuesday	Wednesday	Thursday	Friday	Saturday
			1	2	3	4
5	6	7	8	9	10	11
12	13	14	15	16	17	18
19	20	21	22	23	24	25
26	27	28	29	30		

1. _____

2. _____

3. _____

4. _____

5. _____

6. _____

7. _____

8. _____

9. _____

10. _____

11. _____

12. _____

Now say the answers.

II. Listen. Circle the correct answer.

Example: **a.** Yes, I can.
          b. I leave at 2 today.

1. **a.** Yes. What time?
   b. I take my vacation in July.

2. **a.** I have a day off next week.
   b. I have to ask my husband. I'll tell you after lunch.

3. **a.** I don't know. Can I tell you tomorrow?
   b. I go to lunch at 12.

4. **a.** I need to change my hours.
   b. No, I'm sorry I can't. I don't have a ride.

5. **a.** I think so. I'll tell you tonight.
   b. I have a break at 7:30.

Application

1. **Do you have a schedule at work? Bring in a copy of your work schedule. Tell your class about it.**

2. **Do you sometimes change your schedule? Why?**

   - What do you say?

   - What does your boss say?

   Practice a conversation with a partner. Present your conversation to the class.

Lesson 6   Being on Time

Lena is late for work. She talks to her supervisor.
Listen to the conversation.

Mr. Rice: Why are you late?

Lena: I'm sorry, Mr. Rice. I missed the bus.

Mr. Rice: You were late yesterday, Lena. Your shift starts at 7 o'clock. It's important to be on time.

Lena: I know, Mr. Rice. I'll get the early bus.

Mr. Rice: OK. If there is a problem, you need to call. Leave a message if I'm not at my desk.

Lena: OK, Mr. Rice. Thank you

Are you sometimes late for work? What happens?

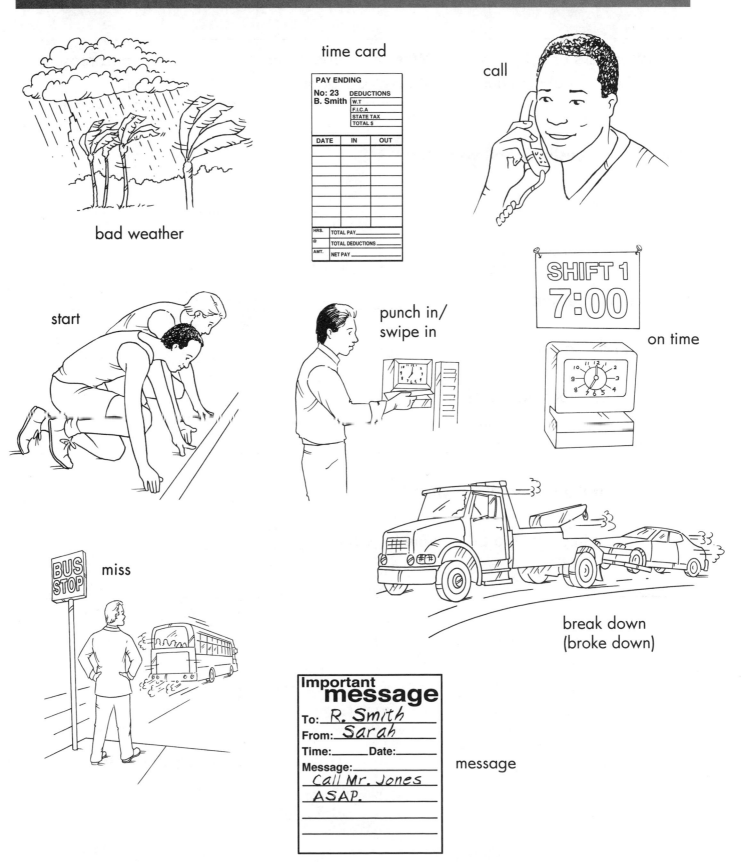

bad weather

time card

call

start

punch in/
swipe in

SHIFT 1
7:00

on time

miss

break down
(broke down)

Important message
To: R. Smith
From: Sarah
Time:_____ Date:_____
Message:_____
Call Mr. Jones
ASAP.

message

Who asks about people	**When** asks about time	**Why** asks for a reason
What asks about things	**Where** asks about place	(because)

Answer the questions. Tell your class.

1. Who is your boss? _____

2. Who do you work with? _____

3. What is your job? _____

4. When do you start work? _____

5. When are your days off? _____

6. Where do you work? _____

7. Where is the lunchroom at work? _____

8. Why is it important to be on time for work? _____

_____

Oral Practice

I. Say it at work.

a. Sorry I'm late.
Sorry I'm late.
The weather's bad.
Sorry I'm late.

b. I'm going to be late.
I'm going to be late.
My car won't start, and
I'm going to be late.

c. I have a lot to do.
I don't want to be late.
I need to hurry.
My shift starts at eight.

II. Practice the conversation.

A. I'm sorry I'm late. _____ (a) _____.

B. It's important to be on time. _____ (b) _____.

A. OK, _____.
(your boss's name)

(a) 1. I missed the train
2. I got up late.
3. There was a long line in the cafeteria.
4. I didn't look at the clock.
5. My ride was late.

(b) You need to get the early train.
You start work at 7:00.
Lunch is 30 minutes. You have to be back.
You only have a 15 minute break.
Your shift starts at 3:00.

I. Look at these reasons for being late. Are they good reasons? Talk with your class.

- My child is sick.

- I slept late.

- My car broke down.

- The babysitter was late.

- There's a lot of traffic.

- The roads are bad.

- I had to go shopping.

- _____

II. Listen to the story. Answer the questions, and talk with your class.

My name is Leo. Some days I'm a little late for work. My boss gets mad. She looks at my time card. She says, "Your shift begins at 7:00, Leo. You have to punch in at 7, not 7:15. You have to be on time." I don't understand. I'm only 15 minutes late. What's the problem?

- Why is Leo's boss mad?

- Why is it important to be on time for work? Explain.

- Are you sometimes late for work? What does your boss say? Explain.

Application

Look at the pictures and the reasons for being late. Use these reasons, and practice the conversation. Tell why you are going to be late.

I had an accident.

The weather is bad.

My car broke down.

A. _____, this is
　　　　(your boss's name)

_____. I'm going to be late.
　　　　(your name)

B. What's the problem?

A. _____.

B. OK. Get here as soon as you can. Thanks for calling.

Now use other good reasons. Work with your class.

Lesson 7   Staying Home from Work

 **Ho can't go to work today. He is sick. Ho calls his boss. Listen to the conversation.**

Boss: Bill Evans speaking.

Ho: Hello, Mr. Evans. This is Ho Fong. I can't come to work today.

Boss: What's wrong, Ho?

Ho: I have the flu.

Boss: That's too bad. Will you be in tomorrow?

Ho: I don't know. I hope so.

Boss: I hope you feel better, Ho. Call me if you can't come in tomorrow.

Ho: OK. Thanks. I will.

Do you sometimes stay home from work? Why?

backache

broken arm

broken leg

earache

fever

flu

headache

sore throat

stomachache

I	have		we	have
you	have		you	have
he				
she }	has		they	have
it				

Complete the sentences.

Example: He _____has_____ a sore throat.

1. I _____ a fever.

2. You _____ a bad cough.

3. We _____ two children.

4. She _____ a broken arm.

5. I _____ a bad toothache.

6. Hara and Habib _____ the flu.

7. Marta _____ an ear infection.

8. I _____ a terrible headache.

Oral Practice

🎧 **I. Say it at work.**

a. I can't come to work.
I can't come to work.
I have a fever, and
I can't come to work.

b. I have the flu.
I have the flu.
There's so much to do.
But I have the flu.

c. I have to call my boss.
This is what I say,
"I cannot come to work.
I'm very sick today."

**II. Use these reasons, and practice the conversation.
Tell why you can't come to work.**

a sore throat and fever	a bad headache	a backache
a broken arm	a stomachache	the flu

A. _____, this is
(your boss's name)

_____. I can't come to work today.
(your name)

B. What's the problem?

A. I have _____.

B. Will you be in tomorrow?

A. I'm not sure. I'm going to the doctor.

B. Please call me later.

A. OK. I will.

Now use your own reasons. Work with your class.

 **Listen. Circle the correct answer.**

Example: **a.** I have a broken leg.
        b. I have a message.

1. **a.** I have a headache.
   b. I have a vacation.

        3. **a.** Thanks.
           b. I have the flu.

2. **a.** I have an earache.
   b. I don't know.

        4. **a.** No, I won't.
           b. OK.

Let's think about it.

Listen to the story. Answer the questions with your class.

Hara is very sick. She has a fever and a bad cough. She can't go to work today. Hara needs to call her boss. She doesn't like to talk on the phone. Her English isn't good. But Hara has to call in sick.

- Why does Hara need to call her boss?

- Why doesn't Hara like to talk on the phone?

Application

1. **Sometimes you can't go to work because you are sick. Sometimes there are other reasons. Make a list with your class.**

   _____   _____

   _____   _____

   _____   _____

2. **Who do you call when you can't go to work? What do you say? Work with a partner. Make a conversation. Present your conversation to the class.**

3. **Sometimes you have to leave a message.**

   - Listen to the voice mail recording.

   - Now practice leaving messages. Work with your class.

Lesson 8   Getting a Paycheck

Paki talks to Florence in the Human Resources (HR) department about his pay. Listen to the conversation.

> **Florence:** This job pays $9.00 an hour, Paki. You get time and a half for overtime.
> **Paki:** When do I get paid?
> **Florence:** Every Friday.
> **Paki:** Do I get benefits?
> **Florence:** Yes, you get two weeks of vacation a year. You also get five sick days and three paid holidays.
> **Paki:** OK. Thanks.

When do you get paid?

Benefits

Vacation
- 2 weeks
  after 1 year of service
- 3 weeks
  after 5 years of service

Sick Days
- 5 Days
  after 1 year of service

Health Insurance
- $50 week
  Individual Plan
- $90 week
  Family Plan

Day Care
- Free On-site
  Monday through Friday

benefits

ABC CORPORATION
222 PARKWAY DRIVE
P.O. BOX 555
DES MOINES, IA 50309

PAYCHECK

09/08/2006   3244

$ 359.70

PAY ....THREE HUNDRED FIFTY-NINE DOLLARS 70 CENTS

TO
THE
ORDER
OF:

JOHN WATERS
431 CENTER LANE
DES MOINES, IA 50321

AUTHORIZED SIGNATURE

ABC CORPORATION
222 PARKWAY DRIVE
P.O. BOX 555
DES MOINES, IA 50309

JOHN WATERS
431 CENTER LANE
DES MOINES, IA 50321

09/8/2006
Check No. 3244

WEEK ENDING	REGULAR HOURS	OVERTIME HOURS	OTHER	TOTAL HOURS
9/1/2006	40	8		48
YEAR TO DATE	800	50		850

REGULAR PAY	OVERTIME PAY	DEDUCTIONS	TAXES	NET PAY
$400.00	$80.00	$50.30	$70.00	$359.70

paycheck/pay stub/overtime/deductions

Help Wanted

Part Time
20 hrs/wk
Pizza Maker
Experience Req'd
Joe's Delivery
Downtown Area

part-time

holiday

Help Wanted

Full Time
40 hrs/wk
Retail Salesperson
Apply in Person
Marie's Gifts
Town Center Mall

full-time

sick days

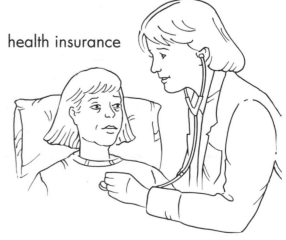

health insurance

Do	I	have	Do	we	have
Do	you	have	Do	you	have
Does	{ he she it }	have	Do	they	have

Complete the questions.

Example: _____Does_____ Ahmed _____have_____ three sick days?
(have)

1. _____ you _____ your paycheck?
(understand)

2. _____ Fay and Pushpa _____ shirts?
(make)

3. _____ Park _____ a computer at work?
(use)

4. _____ I _____ health insurance?
(have)

5. _____ he _____ vacation in July?
(take)

6. _____ we _____ benefits?
(get)

7. _____ I _____ a uniform?
(need)

8. _____ you _____ a headache?
(have)

9. _____ Felipe _____ full-time?
(work)

10. _____ we _____ to lunch at 12?
(go)

Practice the conversation.

A: Excuse me, _____, do you have a minute?

(your boss's name)

B: Sure. What's up?

A: I have a problem with my pay.

B: What's wrong?

A: _____ (a) _____ .

B: OK. I'll check on it for you.

A: Thanks.

(a) 1. I didn't get my overtime this week.
    2. I didn't get my raise.
    3. My hours are wrong.
    4. I didn't get paid for two sick days.
    5. I didn't get my vacation pay.

    6. _____

Let's think about it.

Look at the pay stub. What do you see? Answer the questions.

Name	Ping Fong
Pay Period	12-13-08 – 12-19-08

	Hours	Rate	Total
Regular	40	$8.00	$320.00
Overtime	5	$12.00	$60.00
GROSS PAY ➡			$380.00

Deductions

Fed. Income Tax	$19.00
FICA	$21.20
State Income Tax	$11.50
Health Insurance	$51.00
TOTAL DEDUCTIONS ➡	$102.70
NET PAY ➡	$277.30

1. What is this pay period? _____

2. Does Ping work full-time or part-time? _____

3. What is her overtime pay? _____

4. What are her deductions? _____

_____

_____

5. How much money does Ping take home? _____

Application

1. Answer the questions. Talk with your class.

- Do you work full-time or part-time?
- How many hours a week do you work?
- When do you get paid?
- Do you get a paycheck?
- Do you sometimes have a problem with your paycheck?
  What do you do?

2. Fill in the chart. Tell your class about your benefits.

Benefit	Yes	No	If yes, how many?
Sick days	____	____	_____
Vacation days	____	____	_____
Paid holidays	____	____	_____
Health insurance	____	____	
Education / ESL class	____	____	
Other _____	____	____	_____

Unit Two Check Yourself

	Yes	No	Sometimes
• I understand my schedule.	____	____	____
• I can ask to change my schedule.	____	____	____
• I come to work on time.	____	____	____
• I can call in sick	____	____	____
• I can call in late.	____	____	____
• I understand my paycheck.	____	____	____
• I can talk about my pay.	____	____	____
• I can talk about my benefits.	____	____	____

Lesson 9   Using Safety Gear and Equipment

 **Walter and Viktor work together. They make furniture. They have to wear safety gear. Listen to the conversation.**

Walter: Viktor, where are your safety glasses?

Viktor: They're in my locker.

Walter: You need to get them.

Viktor: But I don't like to wear them.

Walter: You have to wear safety glasses in this department, Viktor. You can hurt your eyes.

Viktor: OK. I'll get them and put them on.

What safety gear do you have at work?

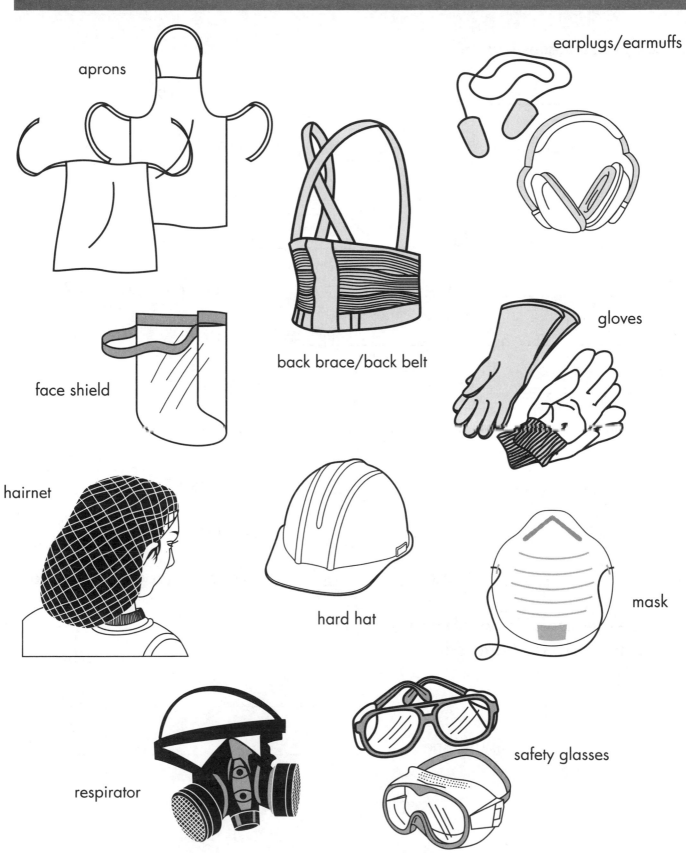

aprons

earplugs/earmuffs

back brace/back belt

gloves

face shield

hairnet

hard hat

mask

respirator

safety glasses

I. Complete the questions.

Example: _____Do_____ you _____have_____ a mask?
(have)

1. _____ he _____ an apron?
(wear)

2. _____ I _____ a hairnet today?
(need)

3. _____ Hana _____ a face shield?
(have)

4. _____ you _____ safety equipment at work?
(use)

5. _____ I _____ a hard hat?
(need)

6. _____ Vera _____ the patients?
(lift)

7. _____ we _____ the tools?
(get)

8. _____ you _____ some earplugs?
(want)

9. _____ they _____ the supplies?
(put away)

10. _____ Maria _____ her safety goggles every day?
(put on)

II. Make questions. Use words from your job.
See page 115 for more verbs.

1. _____ you _____?

2. _____ he/she _____?

3. _____ they _____?

Oral Practice

Practice these conversations with your class.

(1) **A.** Where is your _____(a)_____?

B. I don't know.

A. Go get another one. You need it. It protects your _____(b)_____.

B. OK. Thanks.

(a) apron   (b) body
   back brace   back
   hard hat   head
   face shield   face and eyes
   mask   lungs

_____   _____

_____   _____

(2) **A.** Put on your _____(a)_____?

B. There aren't any more.

A. I'll get some. You need to wear them. They protect your _____(b)_____.

B. You're right. Thanks.

(a) safety glasses   (b) eyes
earmuffs   ears
gloves   hands
boots   feet

_____   _____

Listening Practice

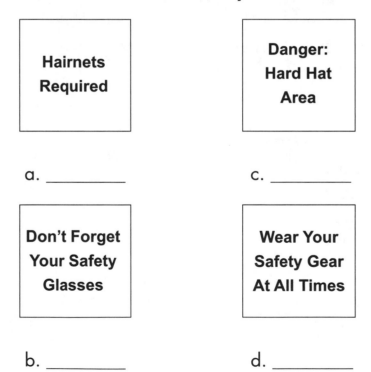 **Listen. Write the number of what you hear under the correct sign.**

Hairnets Required

a. _____

Danger: Hard Hat Area

c. _____

Don't Forget Your Safety Glasses

b. _____

Wear Your Safety Gear At All Times

d. _____

Let's think about it.

 **Listen to the story. Answer the question with your class.**

We had a bad day in the Shipping Department. Haji was lifting heavy boxes. He didn't wear his back brace. He hurt his back.

Now Haji is out of work for two weeks. This is bad for him. This is bad for us, too. We have to do more work.

- Haji didn't wear safety gear. He had an accident. Does this happen where you work? Explain.

Application

1. Do you use safety gear and equipment at work? What do you use? Why do you use it?

2. Do you wear other gear at work? For example, a uniform, a gown, coveralls, a smock, knee pads, etc. Explain.

3. Bring in your safety gear and equipment. Show your class.

Lesson 10 Following Safety Rules

🎧 **Francisco puts boxes in front of an emergency exit. His boss stops him. Listen to the conversation.**

Boss:	Stop! You can't put boxes there.
Francisco:	Why not?
Boss:	That's an emergency exit. You can't put boxes in front of an emergency exit. It's a safety rule.
Francisco:	OK.
Boss:	It's important to follow the safety rules here. Please tell me if you don't understand.
Francisco:	I will.

Are there safety signs and rules where you work?
Do you understand them?

Don't eat or drink here.

Don't touch!/This is hot!

Watch out!/Look out!

Keep out!/Don't go in there.

Don't smoke!/No smoking.

Be careful!

This is very sharp!

Watch your step!

I	don't	understand	we	don't	understand
you	don't	understand	you	don't	understand
he she it }	doesn't	understand	they	don't	understand

Complete the sentences.

Example: She _____doesn't_____ _____understand_____ the sign.
(understand)

1. I _____ _____ a uniform at work.
(wear)

2. Tam _____ _____ a ladder.
(use)

3. Ra and Sam _____ _____ the safety rules.
(know)

4. We _____ _____ good fans in our department.
(have)

5. He _____ _____ the wires.
(touch)

6. You _____ _____ earplugs today.
(need)

7. I _____ _____ the emergency exit.
(see)

8. They _____ _____ their work area.
(clean)

9. You _____ _____ a mask.
(put on)

10. Ramon _____ _____ his tools.
(put away)

Oral Practice

🎧 **I. Say it at work.**

a. Watch out!
Don't touch that pot.
You could get burned.
That pot is hot.

b. Watch your step!
The floor is wet.
You need to be careful.
It's not dry yet.

c. Please be careful
and follow the rules.
You have to put away
all of the tools.

II. Practice the conversation.

A. _____(a)_____ .

B. Why?

A. _____(b)_____ . You could get hurt.

B. OK. Thanks for telling me.

(a) 1. Watch your step.
    2. Be careful.
    3. Don't touch!
    4. Watch out!
    5. Look out!

    6. _____

(b) The floor is wet.
    That knife is very sharp.
    That iron is hot!
    The ladder is falling!
    That cart is moving!

    _____

🎧 **Listen. Write the number of each warning next to the correct sign or picture.**

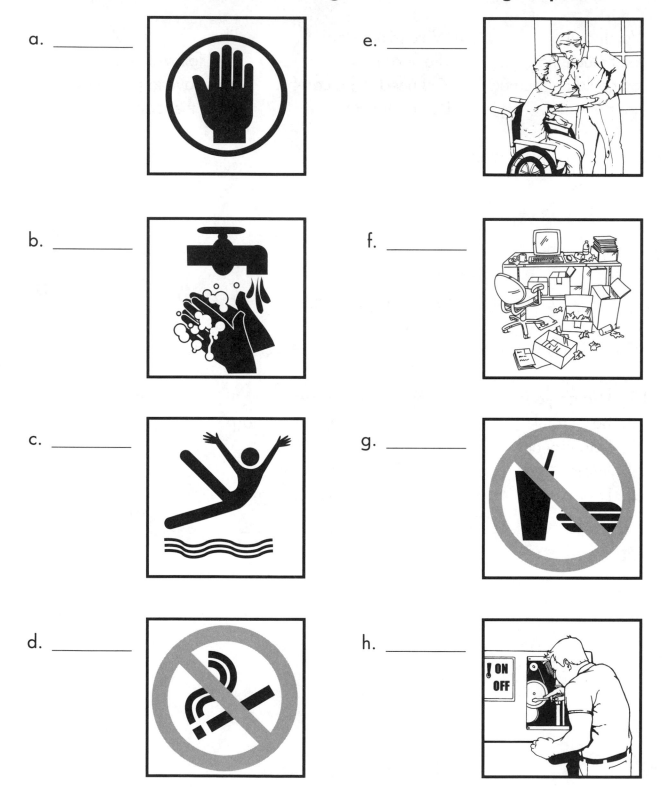

a. _____

b. _____

c. _____

d. _____

e. _____

f. _____

g. _____

h. _____

Emergency Exit	Do Not Enter	Safety Gear Required
Danger	Fire Alarm	Caution
High Voltage	Hazardous Material	Poison

1. What are the safety signs at your job? Make a list with your class. Use words from the signs and your own words.

_____   _____

_____   _____

_____   _____

_____   _____

2. Do you know the safety rules at your job? What are they? Bring your safety rules to class.

3. Do you follow the safety rules at work? Explain.

Joe Rivera reports a safety problem to his manager, Bill Smith. Listen to the conversation.

> **Bill:** Bill Smith speaking.
>
> **Joe:** Bill, we have a problem in the new building.
>
> **Bill:** What's wrong?
>
> **Joe:** There's a leak in the gas pipe. I turned off the gas and called the gas company.
>
> **Bill:** OK, Joe. Make sure everyone is out of the building. I'll be right over.
>
> **Joe:** OK, Bill.

Do you have safety problems at work?

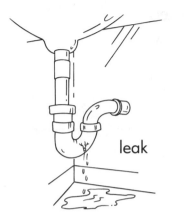

leak

noise/noisy

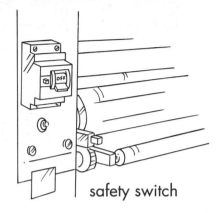

safety switch

bad smell

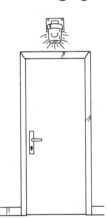

warning light

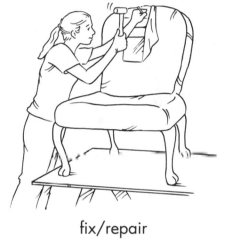

fix/repair

high/low temperature

broken

I	fixed		we	fixed
you	fixed		you	fixed
he she it }	fixed		they	fixed

Complete the sentences with the past tense.

Example: Charlie _____called_____ his supervisor.
(call)

1. Ben _____ the windows.
   (open)

2. Jaco and I _____ the table.
   (move)

3. Faye _____ her hands.
   (wash)

4. We _____ twelve hours on Tuesday.
   (work)

5. I _____ a fire extinguisher yesterday.
   (use)

6. Azi _____ the freezer door.
   (close)

7. Elena _____ the fire alarm.
   (pull)

8. They _____ the leak.
   (fix)

9. I _____ the wires.
   (pick up)

10. Alex _____ the temperature.
    (turn down)

Practice the conversation.

A. _____ speaking.
(your boss's name)

B. Hi, _____. This is
(your boss's name)

_____. There is a problem.
(your name)

A. What's wrong?

B. _____(a)_____.

A. _____(b)_____.

(a) 1. The warning light is on.
2. The safety switch is broken.
3. The meat smells bad.
4. The temperature is too high.
5. I spilled a chemical on the floor.
6. I can't find the HazMat container.
7. The vacuum cleaner is making a noise.

8. _____

(b) Turn off the machine.
Don't turn on the machine.
Don't use it.
Turn off the machine. I'll check it.
Don't touch it. I'll be right there.
OK. I'll get one.
Get another one.

_____

Let's think about it.

There are at least 15 safety problems in the picture. Can you find them?
Can you find others. Work with your class.

1. **Do you have these safety problems at work? Fill in the checklist. Talk with your class.**

	Yes	No	Sometimes
• The light isn't good.	_____	_____	_____
• There is a bad smell.	_____	_____	_____
• There is a lot of noise.	_____	_____	_____
• There is a lot of dust.	_____	_____	_____
• The fan doesn't work.	_____	_____	_____
• There is no fire extinguisher.	_____	_____	_____
• People smoke at work.	_____	_____	_____
• Workers don't clean up.	_____	_____	_____
• Workers use bad equipment.	_____	_____	_____
• People work when they're tired.	_____	_____	_____

2. **Do you report problems at work? Explain.**

3. **Report these safety problems. Work with a partner. Present your conversation to the class.**

   - The smoke alarm is broken. Report it to your boss.
   - There's a spill on the floor in the bathroom. Report it to maintenance.
   - A light in the parking lot is broken. Report it to maintenance.
   - There is no fire extinguisher in your area. Report it to HR.

Lesson 12 Reporting Emergencies

 **Pedro and Sylvia work together. Sylvia burns her arm. Pedro calls the foreman. Listen to the conversation.**

Foreman: Tom Jones speaking.
Pedro: Tom, This is Pedro Rodriguez. Sylvia burned her arm on the stove.
Foreman: Oh, no! What did you do?
Pedro: Sylvia put her arm under cold water. Then I got medicine from the first aid kit. But it's a very bad burn. I think she needs to see a doctor.
Foreman: OK, Pedro. I'll be right there. I'll take her to the hospital.
Pedro: Thanks, Tom. I'll stay with Sylvia.

Can you report emergencies?

bleed/blood

breathe

burn

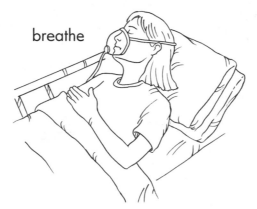

choke

cut

dizzy

fall (fell)

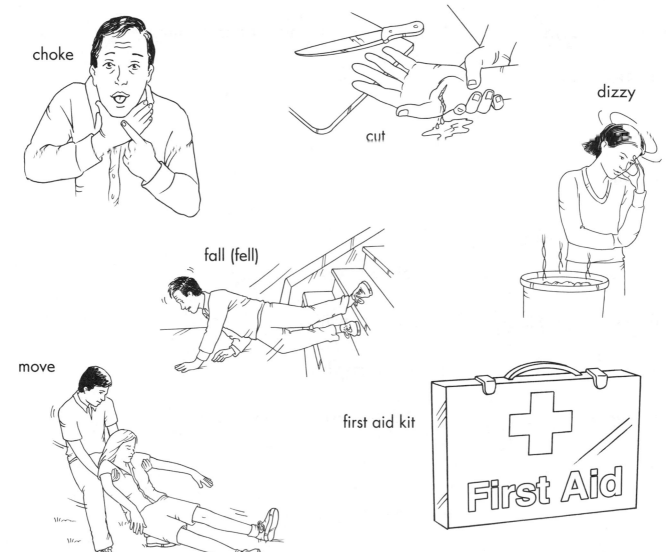

move

first aid kit

Present	Past	Present	Past
cut	cut	go	went
drink	drank	have	had
fall	fell	hurt	hurt
forget	forgot	is, are	was, were
get	got	make	made
give	gave		

Complete the sentences with the past tense.

Example: Tanya _____*cut*_____ cut her finger this morning.
(cut)

1. The children _____ some bleach.
(drink)

2. Beth _____ a bad accident.
(have)

3. She _____ down the stairs.
(fall)

4. I _____ the first aid kit to Sasha.
(give)

5. He _____ a piece of wood in his eye.
(get)

6. There _____ a lot of wires on the floor.
(are)

7. My back _____ yesterday.
(hurt)

8. Lemar _____ to the hospital last week.
(go)

9. We _____ a mistake.
(make)

10. I _____ the emergency number.
(forget)

Oral Practice

Practice the conversation with your class.

A. This is _____.

(your name)

_____ .

(a)

B. Where are you?

A. _____ .

(b)

B. Call 911. I'll be right there.

(a) 1. Tran fell off a ladder. He can't move.
2. Joan cut her arm. She's bleeding a lot.
3. Ruby can't breathe.
4. A big box fell on Ali's foot. He's really hurt.
5. Boo burned his hand with some chemicals.
6. Maria got some metal in her eye.
7. Mrs. Ramos has chest pains.
8. There's a fire on the first floor.

(b) In room 363.
In the packing room.
In the laundry.
In the warehouse.
In the machine shop
In assembly.
In the cafeteria.
In the lobby.

I. Do you know first aid? Can you help in an emergency? Look at the pictures. Tell what to do. Work with your class.

II. Listen to the story. Answer the question and talk with your class.

My name is Jin. I work in a restaurant. I use a lot of oil to cook. Sometimes there is a fire. This is what I do. First I get the fire extinguisher. Next I pull the fire alarm. Then I call my supervisor.

• Do you have emergencies at work? Explain.

1. **What do you do if you have an emergency at work?**

_____

_____

2. **Practice calling 911. Report these emergencies. Work with a partner. Present your conversation to the class.**

 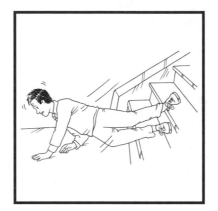

A. 911. What's the emergency?

B. _____.

A. Where are you?

B. _____.
(your work address)

A. Tell me what happened. Speak slowly please.

B. _____.

A. We'll send an ambulance right away.

B. Thank you.

	Yes	No	Sometimes
• I wear safety gear and equipment.	____	____	____
• I understand the safety rules at work.	____	____	____
• I follow the safety rules.	____	____	____
• I understand the signs and safety labels.	____	____	____
• I can find the fire alarms.	____	____	____
• I can find the fire extinguishers.	____	____	____
• I can find the emergency exits.	____	____	____
• I can report emergencies.	____	____	____
• I can find the first aid kit.	____	____	____
• I report safety problems.	____	____	____

Unit Four Working Together

Lesson 13 Reporting Problems and Mistakes

 **George didn't finish his work yesterday. His boss is mad. Listen to the conversation.**

Boss: George, you didn't finish your deliveries yesterday. What happened?

George: I didn't have enough time. I had to help Josef.

Boss: Why didn't you tell me yesterday?

George: I forgot.

Boss: That's no excuse, George. You have to tell me if you can't finish your job. I need to know about any problems.

George: OK.

Do you sometimes have problems at work? Do you report them?

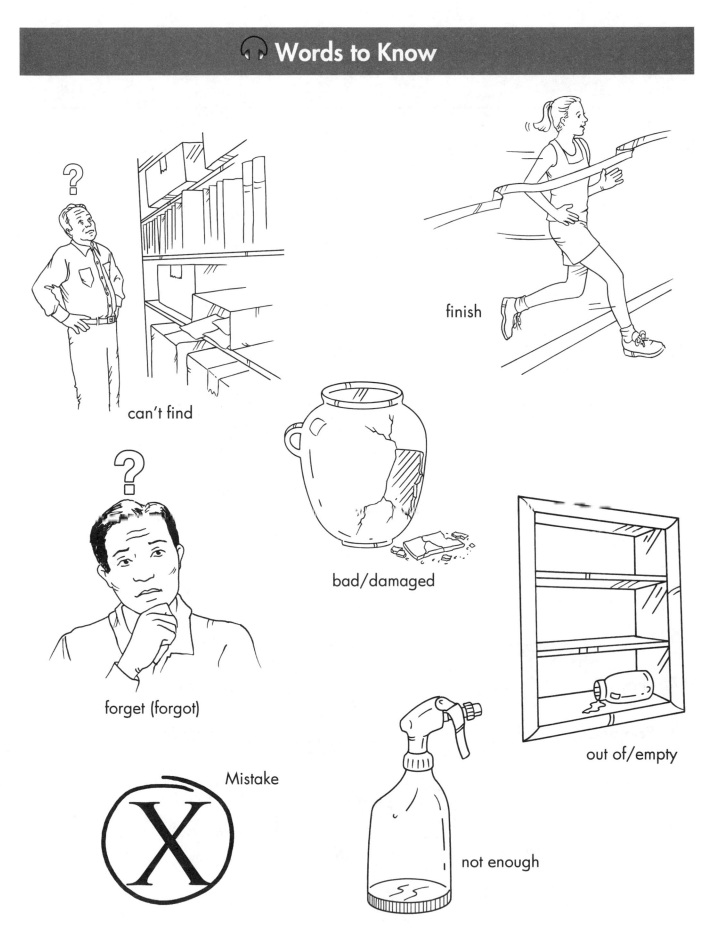

can't find

finish

bad/damaged

forget (forgot)

out of/empty

Mistake

not enough

I	didn't	finish	we	didn't	finish
you	didn't	finish	you	didn't	finish
he she it }	didn't	finish	they	didn't	finish

Complete the sentences.

Example: I _____*didn't*_____ _____*make*_____ the donuts.
(make)

1. You _____ _____ the problem.
(report)

2. We _____ _____ mistakes.
(make)

3. I _____ _____ the directions.
(understand)

4. Patek _____ _____ us.
(help)

5. We _____ _____ the delivery.
(get)

6. I _____ _____ enough time.
(have)

7. They _____ _____ the brushes.
(clean)

8. Boo and I _____ _____ yesterday.
(work)

9. We _____ _____ our work today.
(finish)

10. I _____ _____ to lunch yet.
(go)

Oral Practice

I. Practice the conversation.

A. Have you got a minute?

B. Sure. What's up?

A. _____ (a) _____

B. Thanks for telling me, _____. I'll take care of it.
(your name)

(a) 1. These parts are bad.
   2. We're out of trash bags
   3. These are the wrong directions.
   4. We don't have enough lettuce for the salads.
   5. Mr. Vincent didn't eat his breakfast this morning.
   6. I lost my badge.
   7. I made a mistake. I filled the wrong order.
   8. I forgot the paint.
   9. We didn't get the supplies.

  10. _____.

II. **Use words from your job. Work with your class. Make as many sentences as you can.**

Example: We're out of _____ screws _____.

         These _____ parts _____ are bad.

1. This/These _____ is/are bad.

2. I can't find the _____.

3. There isn't/aren't enough _____.

4. We didn't get the _____.

5. We're out of _____.

6. This is/These are the wrong _____.

Let's think about it.

🎧 **Listen to the story. Answer the question with your class.**

Lidia has a new job. Yesterday her boss told her what to do. Lidia didn't understand everything. But she didn't tell her boss. Lidia made a lot of mistakes. Now she has to report the problems. She has to tell her boss about her mistakes.

• What does Lidia say to her boss? Work with your class. Finish the story.

Application

1. **Do you have these problems at work? Fill in the checklist. Talk with your class.**

	Yes	No	Sometimes
• Not enough supplies	___	___	___
• Wrong shipment or supplies	___	___	___
• Machine is broken	___	___	___
• Damaged or bad materials	___	___	___
• Can't finish the job	___	___	___
• Problems with other workers	___	___	___
• Workers make mistakes	___	___	___

2. **Do you have other problems at work? Talk with your class.**

3. **Who do you talk to when you have a problem (your boss, a friend at work, a union representative, HR, etc.)? Explain.**

4. **Pretend you have a problem at work. Report the problem to your boss.**

   • What do you say?

   • What does your boss say?

Work with a partner. Present your conversation to the class.

Lesson 14   Talking to Co-Workers

 Two workers, Nikki and Patrice, are sitting together in the cafeteria. Listen to their conversation.

Patrice: Hi. My name is Patrice. Are you new here?

Nikki: Yes. This is my first day.

Patrice: What is your name?

Nikki: My name is Nikki.

Patrice: Where are you from, Nikki?

Nikki: I'm from Cambodia.

Patrice: It's nice to meet you. I hope you like it here.

Nikki: Thanks, Patrice. It's nice to meet you, too.

Do you talk to people at work? What do you talk about?

How's your family?

Have a good weekend!

Have a good vacation!

See you on Monday.

Have a nice day!

How's your job?

See you later.

Nice to meet you.

Did	I	have	Did	we	have
Did	you	have	Did	you	have
Did	{ he she it }	have	Did	they	have

Complete the sentences.

Example: _____Did_____ you _____have_____ a good vacation?

(have)

1. _____ you _____ to a party?

(go)

2. _____ your son _____ soccer on Saturday?

(play)

3. _____ Ana _____ a lot of food?

(cook)

4. _____ it _____ last night?

(rain)

5. _____ you _____ a nice weekend?

(have)

6. _____ I _____ enough coffee?

(make)

7. _____ they _____ a new car?

(buy)

8. _____ you _____ time off?

(take)

9. _____ Dang _____ her family in Thailand?

(call)

10. _____ we _____ raises?

(get)

Oral Practice

I. Say it at work.

a. Close the door.
Turn off the light.
See you tomorrow.
Have a good night.

b. How's it going?
Great! How about you?
I'm very busy.
There's so much to do.

c. Did you have a good weekend?
Yes, did you?
No, I was sick.
I had the flu.

II. Practice the conversation with a partner.

A. Hi, _____. How's it going?
(partner's name)

B. Fine, thanks, _____.
(name)

A. _____(a)_____?

B. _____(b)_____. How about you?

A. Same here. See you later, _____.
(partner's name)

B. OK, _____. See you later.
(name)

(a) How's work?
How are you?
How was your weekend?
How was your vacation?

(b) Not bad.
Fine, thanks.
Pretty good.
Great.

_____   _____

Listening Practice

🎧 **Listen. Circle the correct answer. Work with your class.**

1. **a.** See you on Monday.
   b. Good. Thanks for asking.

2. **a.** Thanks. You too.
   b. Pretty good.

3. **a.** Yes I did, thanks.
   b. Nice to meet you.

4. **a.** OK. Have a nice evening.
   b. How about you?

Let's think about it.

🎧 **Listen to the story. Answer the question with your class.**

My name is Marta. I come from El Salvador. My husband and I came to the U.S. six months ago. I want to meet people in this country. I want to make friends at work. But my English is not very good. I am afraid to talk.

• Do you talk to people at work? Explain.

1. **Make your own conversations. Work with a partner. Present your conversations to the class.**

   • Two people meet each other for the first time at work. What do they say?

   • Two workers have a coffee break together. They ask each other about their families (husband, wife, children, mother, father, brother, sister). What do they say?

   • It's Monday morning. Two friends ask each other about the past weekend. What do they say?

2. **Tell the class about your country (weather, food, people, holidays, etc.).**

3. **Talk to someone at work.**

   • Ask about his/her country (name, location, weather food, holidays, etc.)

   • Ask about his/her family (number of people, where they live, their names, etc.).

   • Ask what he/she likes to do.

   Now tell your class about this person.

Lesson 15   Asking for and Giving Help

Fatima and Jean work together. Fatima asks Jean for help. Listen to the conversation.

Fatima: Sorry to bother you, Jean, but can you please help me?

Jean: I can try. What's the matter?

Fatima: I can't read this work order.

Jean: I have to finish something, Fatima. I can help you in a few minutes. OK?

Fatima: That's fine, Jean. Thanks a lot.

Jean: You're welcome.

Who helps you at work?

Can you help me?

Sorry to bother you.

Can I help you?

in an hour

I don't know how.

in a few minutes

in a few minutes	next week	this afternoon
in an hour	now	tomorrow

Complete the sentences with the correct time word or phrase.

Example: It's 9:00. I have a break at 10:00.

I have a break _____ in an hour _____.

1. It's 10:00 AM. I can help you at 3:00 PM today.

   I can help you _____.

2. My shift starts at 7:00. It is 6:53.

   My shift starts _____.

3. I go to lunch at 12. It is 12.

   I go to lunch _____.

4. This is the first week in October. I start my new job the second week in October.

   I start my new job _____.

5. Today is Monday. I can help you on Tuesday.

   I can help you _____.

6. It's 2:00. My break is at 3:00.

   My break is _____.

I. Say it at work.

a. Can you please show me?
I don't know how to do this.
Can you please show me?
I really need to know.

b. Thanks for your help.
Thanks for your help.
Now I can do it.
Thanks for your help.

c. Can I help you?
Is there something you need?
Can I get you some water
or something to read?

II. Practice the conversation.

A. Excuse me, I don't know how to do this. Can you please help me?

B. _____ (a)

A. _____ (b)

B. OK. I'll try.

A. Thanks a lot.

(a) 1. I don't have time.
2. I have my own work to do.
3. No, I'm too busy.

_____

(b) Can you help me later?
Can you get someone else to help me?
I'm sorry to bother you. But I really need help.

_____

Let's think about it.

I. Listen to the story. Answer the questions with your class.

My name is Olga. I work at the Four Star Nursing Home. I check the patients. I ask, "Can I get you something?" Sometimes they want a drink. Sometimes they need a blanket. I get them what they need. I like to help the patients. It makes me feel good.

• How does Olga help people at work?

• Does Olga like to help people?

• Do you help people at work? What do you say?

II. Practice the conversation. Use words from your job. Work with a partner. Present your conversation to the class.

A. Can I help you?

B. _____ (a)

A. _____ (b)

B. Thank you?

A. No Problem

(a) Yes, I can't find the _____

    I don't know how to _____

    I can't read the _____

(b) OK. I'll get it/them.

    I'll show you.

    I'll help you.

Application

1. **Do you need help at work?**

	Yes	No	Sometimes
• Using equipment, tools, etc.	____	____	____
• Lifting things, people	____	____	____
• Finding things, places, people	____	____	____
• Reading orders, rules, etc.	____	____	____
• Reading signs, labels, etc.	____	____	____
• Understanding directions	____	____	____
• Understanding conversations	____	____	____
• Filling out forms	____	____	____
• Understanding benefits	____	____	____
• _____	____	____	____

2. **Do you ask your boss for help? Why or why not? What do you say?**

3. **Do you ask other workers for help? Why or why not? What do you say?**

Maria talks to her supervisor about her work. Listen to the conversation.

Supervisor: I want to talk to you about your job, Maria. You come to work on time. You always look neat. You help other people. You work hard.

Maria: Thank you, Mr. Jones.

Supervisor: There is one problem. You need to be more careful. You make too many mistakes. You have to check your work.

Maria: OK, Mr. Jones. I will.

Are you a good worker? What do you think? What does your boss say?

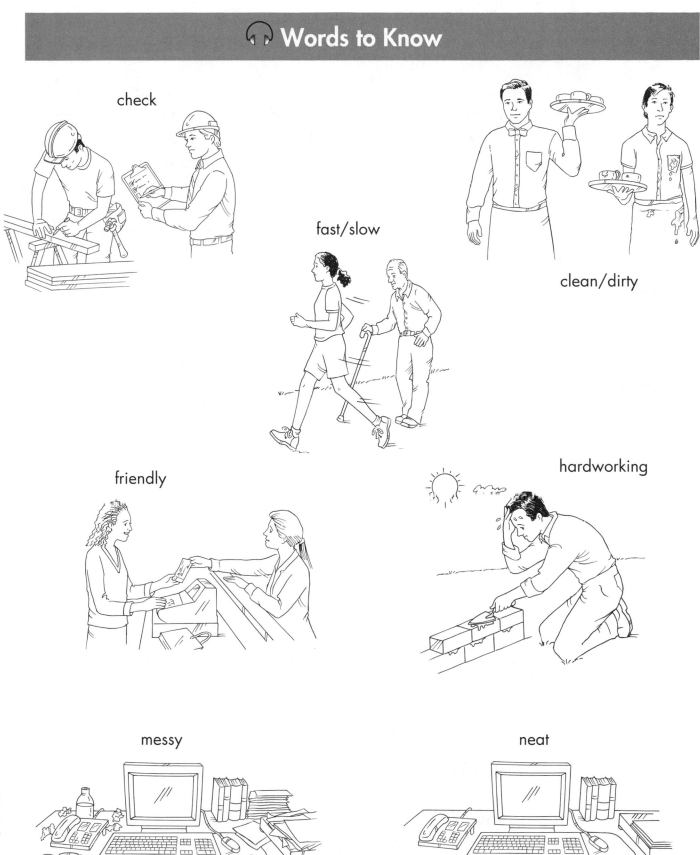

check

fast/slow

clean/dirty

friendly

hardworking

messy

neat

careful	careless	hardworking	lazy
clean	dirty	high	low
early	late	neat	messy
easy	hard	right	wrong
fast	slow	safe	dangerous

Complete the sentences with the correct adjective.

Example: The floor isn't clean. It's _____dirty_____.

1. This job isn't easy. It's _____.

2. This order isn't right. It's _____.

3. Ali isn't lazy. He's _____.

4. The temperature isn't high. It's _____.

5. This chemical isn't safe. It's _____.

6. The machine isn't fast. It's _____.

7. We aren't late. We're _____.

8. These sheets aren't dirty. They're _____.

9. You are not a careful worker. You're _____.

10. Your work area isn't neat. It's _____.

Practice the conversation.

A. Excuse me, _____, _____(a)_____.
(your boss's name)

B. _____(b)_____

A. OK. Thanks.

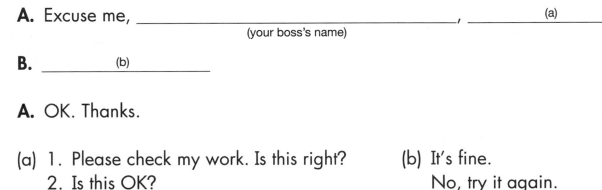

(a)		(b)
1.	Please check my work. Is this right?	It's fine.
2.	Is this OK?	No, try it again.
3.	Am I doing a good job?	Yes, you are.
4.	Did I do this right?	No, let me show you.
5.	I finished my work. What should I do?	Start the next order.
6.	_____	_____

Listening Practice

🎧 **Listen to the supervisor. What would you say?**
Circle the correct answer.

1. **a.** I can't.
   b. OK, I'll try.

2. **a.** I'll try.
   b. I don't want to.

3. **a.** I don't like to.
   b. OK. I will.

4. **a.** OK, I'll wash it.
   b. I don't have enough time to wash it.

Let's think about it.

🎧 **Listen to the story. Answer the questions with your class.**

My name is Gloria. I came to the U.S. six months ago. My job is OK. But I want to make more money. I need to learn more English so I can get a better job.

• Does Gloria want a better job? Why?

• How can Gloria get a better job? What do you think?

Application

1. **Tell the class why you are a good worker. For example, are you neat, helpful, friendly, fast, careful, etc.?**

   I am a good worker. I am _____, _____,

   and _____.

2. **Does your boss talk to you about your work? What does he say?**

   _____

   _____

   _____

   What do you say?

   _____

   _____

   _____

   Work with a partner. Make a conversation between a boss and a worker. Present your conversation to the class.

3. **Do you want a different job? What are your skills?**

   I can _____

   _____

   _____

Unit Four Check Yourself

	Yes	No	Sometimes
• I speak English at work.	____	____	____
• I greet people and introduce myself.	____	____	____
• I report problems.	____	____	____
• I ask for help.	____	____	____
• I ask my boss to check my work.	____	____	____
• I talk to co-workers.	____	____	____
• I talk to customers, patients, guests, etc.	____	____	____
• I am helpful.	____	____	____
• I am a hard worker.	____	____	____
• I finish my work on time every day.	____	____	____

UNIT 1
Lesson 1
Listening Practice (page 10)

Listen to the questions. Write your answers.

1. What is your zip code?
2. What is your area code?
3. What is your date of birth?
4. What is your phone number at work?

Lesson 2
Listening Practice (page 16)

Look at the map on p.15. Listen to the directions. Where are you? Circle the correct answer.

Example: It's on the first floor, across from the meeting room.
   (a. the telephone)   b. the kitchen.
1. It's on the first floor, next to the kitchen.
2. It's on the second floor, near the stairs.
3. It's on the first floor, next to the information desk.
4. It's on the second floor, across from the elevator.
5. It's on the second floor, across from Room 233.
6. It's on the first floor, near the coffee shop.

Lesson 3
Listening Practice (page 22)

Listen to the directions. Repeat them in the same order.

1. Get the coffee pot. Put in the water. Add the coffee.
2. Clean the bathroom. Make the bed. Vacuum the floor.
3. Put the clothes in the washing machine. Add the soap. Turn on the machine.
4. Pick up the package. Put it on the hand truck. Take it to shipping.

Lesson 4
Listening Practice (page 29)

Look at the supply closet on page 27. Listen to the descriptions. Circle the correct answer.

Example: It's on the floor, in front of the pail.
   a. the bleach   (b. the mop)
1. It's on the second shelf, next to the brushes.
2. It's on the second shelf, below the soap.
3. It's on the bottom shelf, in front of the detergent.
4. They're on the top shelf, between the sponges and glasses.

UNIT 2
Lesson 5
Listening Practice I (page 36)

Listen. Write what you hear.

1. Tuesday
2. 2008
3. 13
4. 30
5. 12:15
6. 1985
7. Friday
8. April 26
9. 2012
10. 11:30
11. July 13, 1933
12. Thursday, February 16

Listening Practice II (page 37)

Listen. Circle the correct answer.

Example: Can you work on Saturday?
   (a. Yes, I can.)   b. I leave at 2 today.
1. Can you come in early tomorrow?
2. Can you stay late today?
3. Can you work for Keith on Friday?
4. Can you come in at 7 tomorrow?
5. Can you work this weekend?

Lesson 7

Listening Practice (page 48)

Listen. Circle the correct answer.

Example: What's the problem?
(a. I have a broken leg.)　b. I have a message.

1. What's wrong?
2. Do you think you'll be in tomorrow?
3. Hope you feel better.
4. Call me later.

Application (page 49)

Sometimes you have to leave a message. Listen to the voice mail recording. Follow the instructions in your book.

This is Harry Horton. I'm away from my desk.

Please leave me a message, and I'll call you back.

UNIT 3
Lesson 9

Listening Practice (page 62)

Listen. Write the number of what you hear under the correct sign.

1. You have to wear a hard hat in this area.
2. Put on your safety glasses. You don't want to hurt your eyes.
3. Go get a hairnet. You have to wear it near this machine.
4. Safety gear is required in this department. You have to wear it every day.

Lesson 10

Listening Practice (page 68)

Listen. Write the number of each warning next to the correct sign or picture.

1. Don't forget to clean up before you leave.
2. Watch out! The floor is wet.
3. Be careful. Turn off that machine.
4. You can't eat in here.
5. Wash your hands before you return to work.

6. Be careful. Use the brake.
7. You can't smoke in here.
8. Stop! You can't go in there.

UNIT 4
Lesson 14

Listening Practice (p. 94)

Listen. Circle the correct answer. Work with your class.

1. How's your family?
2. Have a nice weekend.
3. Did you have a good holiday?
4. See you tomorrow.

Lesson 16

Listening Practice (page 106)

Listen to the supervisor. What would you say? Circle the correct answer.

1. You make mistakes. You need to be careful.
2. You're too slow. You need to work faster.
3. You need to ask questions when you don't understand.
4. Your uniform is dirty. It needs to be clean.

Answer Key

UNIT ONE
Lesson 1
Language Practice, p. 8

1. is   He's
2. are   They're
3. are   We're
4. is   She's
5. is   It's
6. am   I'm
7. are   You're
8. is   He's

Lesson 2
Language Practice, p.14

1. Are   6. Are
2. Is   7. Is
3. Are   8. Is
4. Are   9. Is
5. Is   10. Are

Listening Practice, p.16

1. a   4. b
2. a   5. a
3. b   6. b

Let's think about it., p.17

She says, "I'm sorry. I don't understand. They can help you at the Information Desk. It's on the first floor."

Lesson 3
Language Practice, p. 20

1. open   6. closes
2. use   7. put away
3. loads   8. turn off
4. push   9. picks up
5. makes   10. throw away

Lesson 4
Language Practice, p. 26

1. in   5. above
2. below   6. behind
3. on   7. in front of
4. between   8. next to

Listening Practice, p. 29

1. b   3. b
2. b   4. a

UNIT TWO
Lesson 5
Language Practice, p. 34

1. at   6. on
2. from, to 7. from, to
3. on   8. at, in
4. in   9. on
5. on   10. on

Listening Practice I, p. 36

1. Tuesday   7. Friday
2. 2008   8. April 26
3. 13   9. 2012
4. 30   10. 11:30
5. 12:15   11. July 13, 1933
6. 1985   12. Thursday, February 16

Listening Practice II, p. 37

1. a   4. b
2. b   5. a
3. a

Lesson 6
Language Practice, p. 40

Answers will vary.

Let's think about it. II, p.42

- Leo is late for work.

Lesson 7
Language Practice, p. 46

1. have
2. have
3. have
4. has
5. have
6. have
7. has
8. have

Listening Practice, p. 48

1. a
2. b
3. a
4. b

Let's think about it., p. 48

- She can't go to work. She is sick.
- Her English isn't good.

Lesson 8
Language Practice, p. 52

1. Do, understand
2. Do, make
3. Does, use
4. Do, have
5. Does, take
6. Do, get
7. Do, need
8. Do, have
9. Does, work
10. Do, go

Let's think about it., p. 54

1. Dec 13, 2008 to Dec 19, 2008
2. full-time
3. $60
4. Federal Income Tax – $19
   FICA – $21.20
   State Income Tax – $11.50
   Health Insurance – $51
   Total deductions – $102.70
5. $277.30

UNIT THREE
Lesson 9
Language Practice, p. 60

1. Does, wear
2. Do, need
3. Does, have
4. Do, use
5. Do, need
6. Does, lift
7. Do, get
8. Do, want
9. Do, put away
10. Does, put on

Listening Practice, p. 62

a. 3
b. 2
c. 1
d. 4

Lesson 10
Language Practice, p. 66

1. don't wear
2. doesn't use
3. don't know
4. don't have
5. doesn't touch
6. don't need
7. don't see
8. don't clean
9. don't put on
10. doesn't put away

Listening Practice, p. 68

a. 8
b. 5
c. 2
d. 7
e. 6
f. 1
g. 4
h. 3

Lesson 11
Language Practice, p. 72

1. opened
2. moved
3. washed
4. worked
5. used
6. closed
7. pulled
8. fixed
9. picked up
10. turned down

Let's think about it., p. 74

- Uncovered hazmat (toxic material) containers with escaping fumes
- broken stair rail
- empty first aid box
- screwdriver on floor
- boxes in front of emergency exit (blocking exit)
- uncovered/unprotected table saw (no guard on blade)
- scraps of wood on table
- frayed electrical cord
- unprotected electrical outlet on floor
- broken electrical outlet on wall
- man smoking in No Smoking area
- mop on floor
- spill on floor
- cord/plug on floor near spill
- woman looks tired/sick
- woman is not using safety glasses
- woman's hair is long, close to machine, uncovered/loose
- bracelet can get caught in machine
- woman is not wearing gloves
- woman's hands in dangerous position

Lesson 12

Language Practice, p. 78

1. drank	6. were
2. had	7. hurt
3. fell	8. went
4. gave	9. made
5. got	10. forgot

UNIT FOUR
Lesson 13

Language Practice, p. 86

1. didn't report	6. didn't have
2. didn't make	7. didn't clean
3. didn't understand	8. didn't work
4. didn't help	9. didn't finish
5. didn't get	10. didn't go

Lesson 14

Language Practice, p. 92

1. Did, go	6. Did, make
2. Did, play	7. Did, buy
3. Did, cook	8. Did, take
4. Did, rain	9. Did, call
5. Did, have	10. Did get

Listening Practice, p. 94

1. b	3. a
2. a	4. a

Lesson 15

Language Practice, p. 98

1. this afternoon	4. next week
2. in a few minutes	5. tomorrow
3. now	6. in an hour

Let's think about it., p. 100

- She gets them what they need (a drink, a blanket).
- Yes.

Lesson 16

Language Practice, p. 104

1. hard	6. slow
2. wrong	7. early
3. hardworking	8. clean
4. low	9. careless
5. dangerous	10. messy

Listening Practice, p. 106

1. b	3. b
2. a	4. a

Let's think about it., p. 106

- Yes. She wants to make more money.
- She needs to learn more English. (Students should suggest additional answers.)

assembler

babysitter

baker

barber

bricklayer

bus driver

busboy/busperson

butcher

caregiver

carpenter

cashier

certified nurse's assistant (CNA)

child care worker

cleaner

construction worker

cook

delivery person

dishwasher

electrician

factory worker

farmer

fisherman

florist

food server

fruit picker

gardener

gas station attendant

grocery clerk

hairdresser

handyman

home health aide

housekeeper

kitchen worker

landscaper

laundry worker

machine operator

mail room clerk

maintenance worker

manager

manicurist

mason

meat packer

mechanic

mover

musician

nanny

nurse's aide

packer

painter

parking attendant

plumber

repair person

restroom attendant

roofer

salesclerk

sander

shipping clerk

shoe repair person

stitcher

store clerk

taxi driver

technician

truck driver

waiter/waitress

welder

window washer

ask	make
be	miss
break	move
bring	need
burn	open
call	operate
change	pay
check	pick (up)
chop	plug in
clean (up)	pull
close	punch (in/out)
come	push
cook	put (away/on)
cut (up)	read
deliver	repair
do	see
dust	set (up)
fall	speak
feel	spell
fill (out)	start
find	take
finish	talk
fix	tell
forget	think
get	throw (away/out)
give	turn (down/off/on/up)
go	understand
have	unload
help	unplug
hope	use
hurt	want
keep	wash
leave	watch
lift	wear
load	wipe (off/up)
look	

Useful Words • Safety Equipment

apron
back belt
back brace
earplugs/ear muffs
face shield
gloves
goggles

hairnet
hard hat
knee pads
mask
respirator
safety boots/shoes
safety glasses

Useful Words • Safety Signs and Warnings

Caution
Caution — Wet Floor
Danger
Do Not Enter
Do Not Operate Machine
Do Not Touch
Emergency Exit
Fire Alarm (Pull)
Fire Extinguisher
First Aid
Flammable
Harmful If Swallowed
Hazardous Material
High Voltage

Hot Surface
Keep Area Clean
Keep Hands Away
Keep Out
No Food or Drink
No Smoking
Out of Order
Poison
Safety Gear required at all times
Slippery When Wet
Toxic
Wash hands before returning to work
Watch Your Step

I don't understand.
Can you help me?
Can I help you?
Please repeat that.
Please talk slower.
Where is _____?
Where are _____?

Can you work for me on _____?
Can I take my break (now)?
Can I go to lunch (now)?
I can't come to work today. I have a _____.
Can I please have _____ off?
Can I take my vacation _____?
I'm going to be late.
I'm sorry I'm late.

Can you fix this?
The machine broke down.
The warning light is on.
Be careful!
Watch out!
Watch your step!
Stop!
Don't touch.
Clean up _____.
Keep out!

I have a problem.
I have a problem with _____.
I made a mistake.
I forgot (to) _____.
I didn't finish _____.
I can't find _____.
I need more _____.
There isn't/aren't enough _____.
The _____ is broken.
This/these is/are the wrong _____.

Excuse me.
Can I talk to you?
I'm sorry.
What's up?
No problem.
Is this right?
Can I use _____?
Do you have _____?

What country are you from?
Where are you from?
What's your name?
Please.
Thank you.
OK.
Nice meeting you.

Have a nice day.
Have a good weekend/vacation.
See you tomorrow.
See you later.
How's your family?
How was your weekend/vacation?
Did you have a good holiday?

Use these blank pages to write other useful words and expressions for work.

_____

_____

_____

_____

_____

_____

_____

_____

_____

_____

_____

_____

_____